A HOBBY OF MINE

Rishi Dastidar is a fellow of The Complete Works, and a consulting editor at *The Rialto*. His third collection, *Neptune's Projects* (Nine Arches Press) was longlisted for the 2023 Laurel Prize. He is editor of *The Craft: A Guide to Making Poetry Happen in the 21st Century* (Nine Arches Press), and co-editor of *Too Young, Too Loud, Too Different: Poems from Malika's Poetry Kitchen* (Corsair). He reviews poetry for *The Guardian* (UK) and is chair of international writing magazine *Wasafiri*.

Also by Rishi Dastidar

Neptune's Projects	(Nine Arches, 2024)
Supercutscene	(Legitimate Snack, 2021)
Saffron Jack	(Nine Arches, 2020)
The break of a wave	(Offord Road Books, 2019)
Ticker-Tape	(Nine Arches, 2017)

As editor
The Craft: A Guide to Making Poetry Happen in the 21st Century
(Nine Arches, 2019)

As co-editor
You've got too many machines, Richard!: an anthology of Aphex Twin poetry
[with Aaron Kent] (Broken Sleep Books, 2022)
Too Young, Too Loud, Too Different: Poems from Malika's Poetry Kitchen [with Maisie Lawrence] (Corsair, 2021)

© 2025, Rishi Dastidar. All rights reserved; no part of this book may be reproduced by any means without the publisher's permission.

ISBN: 978-1-917617-00-0

The author has asserted their right to be identified as the author of this Work in accordance with the Copyright, Designs and Patents Act 1988

Cover designed by Aaron Kent

Edited and Typeset by Aaron Kent

Broken Sleep Books Ltd
PO BOX 102
Llandysul
SA44 9BG

A hobby of mine

Rishi Dastidar

Broken Sleep Books

A hobby of mine is clicking 'accept all cookies' on a webpage.

A hobby of mine is calling my friends from the pub to tell them I love them.

A hobby of mine is getting 87% of the questions on Richard Osman's House of Games almost right.

A hobby of mine is kvetching.

A hobby of mine is denying I read and take to heart what the co—Star app tells me.

A hobby of mine is making aggressive use of the language meme 'in this essay I will'.

A hobby of mine is being next man up in undangerous situations.

A hobby of mine is dreaming of cheese rolling down Gloucestershire hills.

A hobby of mine is drafting thought leadership pieces I will never post on LinkedIn.

A hobby of mine is saying "I could have been the Casanova of the 21st century."

A hobby of mine is saying yes.

A hobby of mine is apertivo.

A hobby of mine is saying yes to a second negroni.

A hobby of mine is pressing my nose up against the telly.

A hobby of mine using the world 'telly' even though that implies a device with a cathode-ray tube and a bulge in front rather than a flat screen.

A hobby of mine is bugling.

A hobby of mine is constructing entries for a modern *Devil's Dictionary*: "copywriting (adv): the act of attempting to sell the unnecessary to the unwashed with unspeakable language."

A hobby of mine is claiming things as brands. "Look closely, and this runcible spoon becomes a brand."

A hobby of mine is posting.

A hobby of mine is arranging myself so the cat is more comfortable on the duvet than I am under it.

A hobby of mine is arranging myself so the car is more comfortable on the driveway than I am under it.

A hobby of mine is never remembering my dreams except one.

A hobby of mine is coughing when I wake up.

A hobby of mine is the letter 'a'.

A hobby of mine is pointing out to people that when they say they preferred a band's earlier music, what they're really saying is they preferred their younger selves and lives then.

A hobby of mine is trying to explain the difference between coincidence and serendipity, to myself mostly, but passing others sometimes.

A hobby of mine is to say 'AN HOBBY' loudly in situations I probably shouldn't.

A hobby of mine is to do similar in citations.

A hobby of mine is re-reading the messages I've starred in WhatsApp.

A hobby of mine is not leaving certain WhatsApp groups then seething as I realise I've not put them on mute.

A hobby of mine is seething.

A hobby of mine is playing dodgeball with viruses and failing.

A hobby of mine is parsing sensibilities for their ideological fixations.

A hobby of mine is berating people for their ideological fixations.

A hobby of mine is not playing Tetris when I should.

A hobby of mine is trying out new social networks and eventually always coming back to the one I shouldn't use any more.

A hobby of mine is launching a memory into orbit and waiting for it to drift gently back to the desert I'm waiting in.

A hobby of mine is pretending the right person is a swipe away.

A hobby of mine is falling in love.

A hobby of mine is falling out of love.

A hobby of mine is doing the above two hobbies in the wrong order.

A hobby of mine is using 'dooberry' as all-purpose noun and adjective.

A hobby of mine is coming up with titles for other people's books a/k/a writing poems.

A hobby of mine is adding the word 'grasp' as a suffix in proverbs: "a stitch in time saves nine grasps".

A hobby of mine is taking Foghorn Leghorn around America in search of democracy.

A hobby of mine is yearning to be Alexis de Tocqueville.

A hobby of mine is being panicked by hips.

A hobby of mine is perverting the course of language.

A hobby of mine is the habit of mining.

A hobby of mine is wondering what the modern equivalent of mining school in nineteenth century Europe is.

A hobby of mine is running away to Rome.

A hobby of mine is imagining living in the south of France with a large of amount of cash that is demanding to be whittled away.

A hobby of mine is telling people why I haven't launched a Substack yet.

A hobby of mine is deciding which of the endangered heritage crafts I should attempt to pick up.

A hobby of mine is calling the sun my father.

A hobby of mine is sitting in the middle of the road, crying that the passing scooters won't stop and play with me.

A hobby of mine is wishing I was a cat.

A hobby of mine is knowing I would have been a very good clerk for the East India Company.

A hobby of mine is cultivating an emollient aspect to my personality.

A hobby of mine is swapping the word 'unctuous' for 'emollient' in that above statement.

A hobby of mine is claiming I listen to modern classical music, when the reality is that I like the idea of listening to modern classical music more than actually doing it.

A hobby of mine is standing under the transparent swimming pool in the sky in Nine Elms that connects two apartment buildings, and declaring loudly that you'd never catch me swimming in it.

A hobby of mine is not improving my weak swimming skills, or working on my fear of heights.

A hobby of mine is leaving post it notes with obliquely inspiring messages on them: "Write the ghosts".

A hobby of mine is talking about infinity like I know what I'm talking about.

A hobby of mine is taking up new hobbies.

A hobby of mine is taking up new hobbies with one eye to monetising them as part of my side hustles.

A hobby of mine is taking up new hobbies after watching them on the telly.

A hobby of mine is a paranoid fear about not having enough hobbies after watching *Why Don't You?* when growing up, which made me believe that spending time in front of the TV was akin to killing yourself, and I never appreciated the irony of such a message being delivered via a TV programme.

A hobby of mine is elaborate masturbation rituals.

A hobby of mine is denying to myself that these rituals exist.

A hobby of mine is collecting phrases in a notebook, then looking at the pages muttering "what was I thinking?"

A hobby of mine is feeling sad the rest of the world doesn't care for the precise contours of my enthusiasms.

A hobby of mine is shopping for baseball caps I won't actually buy.

A hobby of mine is thinking about the first song for the first dance at our wedding.

A hobby of mine is trying to redefine whimsy for the 21st century.

A hobby of mine is lying about my first memory. I'm pretty sure I've reconstructed it from a photograph of me riding a green tricycle when I was three.

A hobby of mine is creative destruction in situations where I am insulated from the effects of that destruction.

A hobby of mine is insisting that John Torode and Lisa Faulkner are the most under-rated presenting pair on British television.

A hobby of mine is being a man out of time.

A hobby of mine is serving in agencies of all the talents.

A hobby of mine is the futile avoidance of senescence.

A hobby of mine is reading Trollope as part of my regime for the avoidance of senescence.

A hobby of mine is saying "Milady" to my reflection. Sometimes I curtesy.

A hobby of mine is drinking in the shadows.

A hobby of mine is confusing work with play, then feeling sad in the office.

A hobby of mine is carrying a paper bag around all day, long after the point I've needed to, or needed the item the bag originally contained.

A hobby of mine is carrying various items in a plastic bag that is then in turn carried within a tote bag that I might need for a given or more likely unforeseen moment: a pack of tissues, hand sanitizer, a blister of ibuprofen, nasal spray, an aromatherapy stress relieving 'stick' of fragrance that claims it is lavender-based, but has a sickly, chemically undertow to it.

A hobby of mine is picturing my thoughts as miniature hummingbirds, flitting between axons, taking off and landing between the hemispheres of my brain.

A hobby of mine is writing books under the pen name of my cat, Malachite T Boy Cat Esq.

A hobby of mine is throwing my voice so I sound like Bane on phone calls.

A hobby of mine is 'watching' US sports on Sunday nights via social media updates, then digitally shouting at people who claim that doesn't make me a real fan. #HTTC #RingTheBell

A hobby of mine is using the words 'darkly dazzling' in inappropriate contexts: "this is a darkly dazzling Caesar salad" I said at a dinner party once. I wasn't asked back.

A hobby of mine is seeing around corners, then not acting on the information gleaned.

A hobby of mine is thinking in PowerPoint presentations then being surprised that the world is not like a PowerPoint presentation.

A hobby of mine is coming home.

A hobby of mine is being the other person in love triangles.

A hobby of mine is hoping someone agrees when I quote Clemenceau and say: the best moment in love is climbing the stairs.

A hobby of mine is hoping I meet someone who knows who Clemenceau is.

A hobby of mine is hoping I meet anyone who gets any of my references.

A hobby of mine is climbing out of windows when the second person in a love triangle comes home early.

A hobby of mine is building Lego kits for adults and thinking that makes me truly creative rather than skilled at following instructions.

A hobby of mine is telling people younger than me about the times I went out dancing.

A hobby of mine is dancing in the kitchen.

A hobby of mine is aggressively changing the station when *The Archers* comes on.

A hobby of mine is turning houses upside down, for no good reasons.

A hobby of mine is folding my arms over my chest in an unconscious, subconscious tribute to my dad.

A hobby of mine is collecting unopened decks of playing cards.

A hobby of mine is conforming.

A hobby of mine is conforming to the defying of the expectations of conformity.

A hobby of mine is making gestures that can never be reciprocated.

A hobby of mine is treating the lyrics of indie rock songs as proverbs.

A hobby of mine is talking back to the TV like it can hear, or cares.

A hobby of mine is wishing I had disco ball for a heart.

A hobby of mine is misjudging character.

A hobby of mine is wondering why my phone undercounts my steps by at least 590 steps every day.

A hobby of mine is calling a year when our species disappears.

A hobby of mine is recognising game.

A hobby of mine is running the table.

A hobby of mine is inventing colours like Elevator Pink; that's one of mine.

A hobby of mine is collecting relics of the soon to be over age of oil. Or shopping, as it's otherwise known.

A hobby of mine is forgetting.

A hobby of mine is hoping a deus ex machina will change my life, or prayer will be answered, or my lottery numbers will come up; I'm relaxed about whether that all happens in the same week.

A hobby of mine is twiddling with my hair, especially in the presence of someone I don't know I fancy yet.

A hobby of mine is positioning my misanthropy as common sense towards a cruel world.

A hobby of mine is denying my self-obsession would make Narcissus blush. Attractively, of course.

A hobby of mine is promising to change, once I've finished the next drink.

A hobby of mine is painting black sunshine and grey rainbows.

A hobby of mine is inverting optimism.

A hobby of mine is trying to prove my clothes are in conversation about how much they hate being worn by me.

A hobby of mine is putting content that should be tweets into derivative memoir structures.

A hobby of mine is asking: how would David Foster Wallace have written it?

A hobby of mine is attempting to write things the way David Foster Wallace might have done, and failing.

A hobby of mine is buying any second-hand edition of *The Golden Gate* by Vikram Seth I ever see.

A hobby of mine is Tabasco.

A hobby of mine is predicting when money dies.

A hobby of mine is predicting when Miami sinks.

A hobby of mine is thinking up sports entertainment formats for a post-apocalyptic planet.

A hobby of mine is re-litigating the past until it asks to be taken from the courtroom and hanged until it is dead.

A hobby of mine is saying 'wait till next year' even though I know my team will be crap then also.

A hobby of mine is only reading my horoscope when I feel some part of my life is out of control.

A hobby of mine is opening all the cupboards in the kitchen looking for chocolate to eat, even though I know there isn't any in the house.

A hobby of mine is saying "Rump Parliament" through a megaphone out of the living room window.

A hobby of mine is transliterating euphemistic language.

A hobby of mine is ignoring the froth of kings and princes.

A hobby of mine is advocating in favour of the ebb of deep time.

A hobby of mine is gossiping in a way that belies my dignity.

A hobby of mine is announcing "I am good at political analysis, not at politics."

A hobby of mine is jaw-dropping.

A hobby of mine is turning moments of geopolitical statecraft into Ealing comedies. Brexit Galore! The Woman In The Kitten Heels. The Man With All The White Lies.

A hobby of mine is paid employment.

A hobby of mine is compound interest.

A hobby of mine is breaking beats and jumping time.

A hobby of mine is sending clips of thunderbastards to suitably appreciative friends.

A hobby of mine is being present.

A hobby of mine is being President.

A hobby of mine is being presented.

A hobby of mine is guesstimating what your specialist subject on would be *Mastermind*.

A hobby of mine is turning the words of Boogie Down Productions into psalms.

A hobby of mine is upping the ante on new historical epochs. It's not the Daisy Age, it's the Dandelion Age.

A hobby of mine is strictly business.

A hobby of mine is reminding people that *Top Cat* was originally called *Boss Cat* in the UK.

A hobby of mine is reminding people that *Top Cat* was a feline version of *Sgt Bilko*.

A hobby of mine is typing 'a hobby of mind'.

A hobby of mine is listening to hip hop when I'm doing flow work.

A hobby of mine is doing it in the mix.

A hobby of mine is sampling.

A hobby of mine is passing expensive bottles of liqueur in clubs in the hopes a rapper might mention it in a song.

A hobby of mine is being a triple threat.

A hobby of mine is being a model slash actress slash whatever.

A hobby of mine is using the pipes punctuation mark where it's least expected.

A hobby of mine is campaigning for the semi colon.

A hobby of mine is interrogating the interrobang.

A hobby of mine is denying I'm tipsy.

A hobby of mine is vilifying the matador (hi Scott).

A hobby of mine is writing manifestos that declare that pop music that doesn't concentrate on artifice and artificiality as much as the music should not actually be considered as pop music.

A hobby of mine is wondering if we'd autotune Lincoln when he was delivering the Gettysburg Address.

A hobby of mine is losing on the pools.

A hobby of mine is struggling to see the near past.

A hobby of mine is saying any old shit in the hope it makes me look sufficiently ideological so I can go on the telly instead of doing whatever my day job is.

A hobby of mine is filing metaphors in filing cabinets, and similes in container-like boxes.

A hobby of mine is coming up with ideas for logos and designs to put on baseball caps. Here's two: 1) the outline of a top hat; 2) the crest of a fictional US sports team called the Chesapeake Bay Ironsides.

A hobby of mine is coughing first thing in the morning, and fearing this means things are worse.

A hobby of mine is applying for jobs without tailoring my CV.

A hobby of mine is taking ideas into the thought shower and scrubbing them clean.

A hobby of mine is worrying that the headaches are something far worse.

A hobby of mine is wishing for temporary incapacitation that doesn't actually change my life meaningfully.

A hobby of mine is the repair of sleep.

A hobby of mine is finding things to get obsessed about for very short periods of time: 30 minutes, a day, a month at most.

A hobby of mine is writing Onegin sonnets.

A hobby of mine is storyboarding my dreams.

A hobby of mine is being one of Kelly's Heroes or the Magnificent Seven, depending on whim.

A hobby of mine is typing 'becalmed' repeatedly into a note on my phone in an effort to be calm.

A hobby of mine is singing along badly to 'Everything Flows' by Teenage Fanclub. You could put almost any other song title in that formulation. The quality of crooning won't improve. But it's really bad with that one.

A hobby of mine is arguing that "Under neon loneliness / Motorcycle Emptiness" is the truest couplet about the late 20th century.

A hobby of mine is putting Blur's 'To The End' at the end of playlists.

A hobby of mine is saying "BARK, BARK *eyes spinning* MARRY ME NOW hummina hummina AWOOOGA." Out loud. Thanks Heidi.

A hobby of mine is making reality.

A hobby of mine is bending light into a figure of eight.

A hobby of mine is thinking about what I'd do with imaginary lovers in hotel rooms I can't afford.

A hobby of mine is making up silly songs to sing to the cat. Sometimes he responds in a miaowy chitter chatter. More often, he walks away, bemused.

A hobby of mine is being the area poet most attractive to viruses.

A hobby of mine is wandering lonely o'er moonlit mountaintops and fields.

A hobby of mine is trying to spot writers through binoculars.

A hobby of mine is training King Charles spaniels to be able to bark Martin Luther's 95 theses.

A hobby of mine is seeking out bodies kissed by the sun.

A hobby of mine is putting my insides on the outside.

A hobby of mine is writing to reach you.

A hobby of mine is building a time machine out of regrets and string.

A hobby of mine is content farming. Someone has to tend the tendrils of TikToks, the crop of hot takes, fertilise them with love and nonsense.

A hobby of mine is performing life rather than living it.

A hobby of mine is trying to construct Venn diagrams that contain the system of the world.

A hobby of mine is treading softly on your dreams.

A hobby of mine is riding Trojan horses rather than hiding inside them, and oh the scrapes that has got me into!

A hobby of mine is chasing chunky unicorns through a mythos.

A hobby of mine is misreading clouds.

A hobby of mine is my art.

A hobby of mine is pointing out that my art is not actually a hobby but how I sustain myself and nourish and entertain you, and contribute to the wider economy, and gross national happiness.

A hobby of mine is yelling "I beseech you, in the bowels of Christ, think it possible that you may be mistaken" at the radio when a politician is on.

A hobby of mine is existing.

A hobby of mine is attempting to catalogue the types of thoughts, and the frequency of them, much as Howie in Nicholson Baker's *The Mezzanine* attempts, and then repudiates.

A hobby of mine is suggesting to others that that above-named novel would have been better if it consisted solely of the tabulation of Howie's thoughts and the relevant footnotes.

A hobby of mine is to be way more neophiliac than a man in his late 40s should be.

A hobby of mine is to reinvent psychedelia for suburbia.

A hobby of mine is attempting to make my diffidence look attractive.

A hobby of mine is dismissing other people's hobbies.

A hobby of mine is elaborating extemporaneous riffs on marginal and esoteric subjects in the hope that someone will transcribe them into a book.

A hobby of mine is preparing for voyages of exploration and wonder that I won't actually embark upon.

A hobby of mine is using the word 'wanton' in an inappropriate manner: "these crisps are so wanton".

A hobby of mine is regicide.

A hobby of mine is sinking the Titanic again.

A hobby of mine is lowering the Atlantic.

A hobby of mine is recreating the moon landings in my back garden. I play Michael Collins.

A hobby of mine is wolf whistling Cavaliers and snogging Roundheads.

A hobby of mine is letting problems fester until they explode into unjustified anger and stand-up recriminations.

A hobby of mine is tweaking the social connexions between Man.

A hobby of mine is yield management.

A hobby of mine is A/B testing my love language in online focus groups.

A hobby of mine is invoking the Bill of Rights loudly, confidently, and wrongly in disputes with shopkeepers.

A hobby of mine is conspiring with conspirators to conjure conspiracies in conjoined corporations.

A hobby of mine is establishing beachheads into rainforests in order that the cartographers can accomplish their mission with grace and ease.

A hobby of mine is finding me.

A hobby of mine is sitting in my *New Yorker* office and not writing for 40 years.

A hobby of mine is being overwhelmed by the futility of existence.

A hobby of mine is ragu, on top of lightly toasted sliced white bread.

A hobby of mine is translating *Eugene Onegin* into emojis.

A hobby of mine is doomscrolling after fucking.

A hobby of mine is drinking the tears of Julius Caesar while sitting on top of Trajan's column.

A hobbyz of minez iz addingz an unnecezzary z to wordz.

A hobby of mine is saying "And a good moo to you!" to passing herds of cows.

A hobby of mine is rescinding my membership of the reality-based community, then applying to join again in a panic 37 hours later.

A hobby of mine is reading π out loud.

A hobby of mine is thwarting the passion between shop girls and barrow boys.

A hobby of mine is gobbets.

A hobby of mine is arguing that, away from its business successes, IBM as a brand did more to shape post-WW2 creative and civic culture than is recognised, and that its retreat from this corporate leadership has left us all impoverished, and that this state can be traced back to the ascent of shareholder value as the only variety of capitalism to achieve a dominant position in the global economy.

A hobby of mine is working to rule.

A hobby of mine is banging rights to rights.

A hobby of mine is vocalising the *Sportsnight* theme tune in the style of Sammy Davis Jr.

A hobby of mine is being haunted by you.

A hobby of mine is indicting others around me for the crime of farting.

A hobby of mine is living hand to mouth for a time-limited period in order to 'keep it real'.

A hobby of mine is Odessa.

A hobby of mine is marriage.

A hobby of mine is talking dirty in my telephone voice.

A hobby of mine is arranging plainsong versions of punk songs.

A hobby of mine is erasing other people's marginalia.

A hobby of mine is instant gratification.

A hobby of mine is delayed gratification.

A hobby of mine is The Way.

A hobby of mine is The Deep.

A hobby of mine is dancing to both (word to the Global Communication heads).

A hobby of mine is reading an entry of Pepys' diary every day.

A hobby of mine is selling long songs.

A hobby of mine is painting model buses made of cardboard because I want to be a former Prime Minister, apparently.

A hobby of mine is reviving magazines.

A hobby of mine is questioning obedience.

A hobby of mine is prioritising the imagination.

A hobby of mine is sniffing briefcases.

A hobby of mine is finding a way around boulders at the bottom of ravines.

A hobby of mine is touching garlic.

A hobby of mine is mediating the world rather than experiencing it.

A hobby of mine is breaking my legs so I can walk like a clown.

A hobby of mine is giving up my divine status so I can fall in love again then die.

A hobby of yours is reading this.

A hobby of mine is stirring the eternal pot.

A hobby of mine is reconstructing the occupation.

A hobby of mine is freeing corpulent bees from massive spiders' webs.

A hobby of mine is blowing little puffs of steam.

A hobby of mine is constructing High Line urban gardens through the living rooms of suburban homes.

A hobby of mine is putting hot takes into hot pockets for consumption by tepid minds and cool bodies.

A hobby of mine is being a true lucifer.

A hobby of mine is igniting a full box of matches for no reason.

A hobby of mine is letting it all hang loose. Or out. Or down.

A hobby of mine is buttoning everything back up.

A hobby of mine is being opaque about my past, in the hope it makes me appear mysterious rather than boring.

A hobby of mine is roguery.

A hobby of mine is Tom and Jerry-ing around town.

A hobby of mine is being a mid-ranking member of The Fancy.

A hobby of mine is trying to think of equivalents of 'l'Hexagone' for the UK; 'The Isosceles' is still my best attempt.

A hobby of mine is searching for my metier for the third act of my life.

A hobby of mine is losing my claims to respectability and an ordinary life.

A hobby of mine is being one of the great horizontals of the Belle Epoque.

A hobby of mine is throwing up a facade of sobriety and organisation, the better to disguise my swaggering hedonism.

A hobby of mine is luxurious poverty.

A hobby of mine is navigating the anxiety of freedom.

A hobby of mine is coming from a village with a spirit of vengeance.

A hobby of mine is reverting to modernism.

A hobby of mine is collecting apocryphal stories and turning them into SKUs and other economically useful indicators.

A hobby of mine is de-moralising luck as a factor in my modes of living.

A hobby of mine is claiming Prince Rogers Nelson was the reincarnation of Wolfgang Amadeus Mozart.

A hobby of mine is looking for you.

A hobby of mine is spraying clouds of aftershave as I walk into restaurants.

A hobby of mine is being aristocratic and impoverished.

A hobby of mine is being Marianne, the allegory of France.

A hobby of mine is tailoring propaganda to make it palatable.

A hobby of mine is being capricious.

A hobby of mine is wearing a top hat to football matches.

A hobby of mine is keeping ghosts out of the palace.

A hobby of mine is being a very bad dead person.

A hobby of mine is being a self-facilitating media production node.

A hobby of mine is flirting with the person behind the cash till in bookshops.

A hobby of mine is supporting River Plate because I watched them play in El Monumental once.

A hobby of mine is cannibalising myself.

A hobby of mine is waiting for the Philadelphia Phillies to swoon in September.

A hobby of mine is trying to find the guy who did this.

A hobby of mine is writing faux-intellectual screeds to justify heinous behaviour, mine and others.

A hobby of mine is statement wins.

A hobby of mine is adopting a war posture over a self-victualling tablecloth.

A hobby of mine is being crazy and south Asian but not rich.

A hobby of mine is taking my blood, putting it into stanzas in the hope that it might save us. Save me.

A hobby of mine is mimicking intoxication on trace levels of alcohol.

A hobby of mine is biting my tongue after seeing bad plays at the theatre.

A hobby of mine is examining the past through a funhouse mirror.

A hobby of mine is matching sounds from domestic appliances to sounds I've heard in songs. For example, the wheeze the fridge gives out when I open its door sounds exactly like the mid-point (5.12) in the breakdown of 'The Private Psychedelic Reel' by The Chemical Brothers.

A hobby of mine is repeating myself.

A hobby of mine is being curiously unsatisfied. This of course might just be the modern way of things, living in the times we do.

A hobby of mine is writing an oral history of my life to date.

A hobby of mine is repeating myself.

A hobby of mine is being as precious and predictable as Andy Warhol.

A hobby of mine is catching myself repeating myself, and rephrasing the point I was going to make in an effort to suggest that I am not, in actuality, repeating myself.

A hobby of mine is failing to stop myself repeating myself.

A hobby of mine is making you look good on the dance floor.

A hobby of mine is sitting down during a standing ovation.

A hobby of mine is talking to America here.

A hobby of mine is being brittle.

A hobby of mine is pretending everything is confessional, brutally so, when it is merely the surface of things, indiscreet at best.

A hobby of mine is telling people I'm fine when I'm not. But I assume everyone does this. Maybe it is the world's most popular hobby.

A hobby of mine is capturing things for the left: schools, think tanks, quangos, government bodies, central banks, broadcasters, newspapers, cafes, department stores, nurseries, playgrounds.

A hobby of mine is instructing other people to take purity tests that I keep failing.

A hobby of mine is wondering what my late style will be.

A hobby of mine is claiming I'm a good chap who can be trusted to govern.

A hobby of mine is saying things like "oh yes I think his work is Amis-ian" with a straight face.

A hobby of mine is never remotely remembering my dreams no matter how deep or shallow my sleep has been; it's always flat, hard, dull – does nothing happen in my R.E.M.? It appears not.

A hobby of mine is railing against the inevitable and necessary oblivion of my writing, and by extension me, and my sense of self.

A hobby of mine is leaving runners stranded in scoring positions.

A hobby of mine is giving myself a pep talk, when no one else will.

A hobby of mine is separating the private and the public.

A hobby of mine is imagining how I would sabotage my appearances on reality TV programmes.

A hobby of mine is collecting colours in a scrapbook lodged at the back of my eye.

A hobby of mine is the New London Fabulous.

A hobby of mine is cataloguing moments of joy in order to forget them, and free space in my emotional bank.

A hobby of mine is going to bed.

A hobby of mine is getting out of bed.

A hobby of mine is doing the Texas Two-Step.

A hobby of mine is juking when walking down the street.

A hobby of mine is wondering about what Anthony Trollope would be writing about if he was alive today. I like to think he'd add to the Barchester Chronicles with a volume about the efforts of a brand consultant that tried to save the Church of England, through the medium of slide decks proposing ideas like selling branded stained glass windows.

A hobby of mine is crowning the sons of petty kings.

A hobby of mine is playing air slap bass.

A hobby of mine is saying "I could do that" when watching *Strictly Come Dancing*.

A hobby of mine is typing 'mine' as 'Maine'.

A hobby of mine is not thinking but vibing.

A hobby of mine is correcting autocorrect when I want to swear in a message.

A hobby of mine is conquering my hinterland.

A hobby of mine is being biased towards beauty.

A hobby of mine is not noticing everything around me.

A hobby of mine is having meetings that could have been emails.

A hobby of mine is never turning down the chance to meet someone over coffee.

A hobby of mine is working harder than ever and calling it "Macking".

A hobby of mine is feeling gravity.

A hobby of mine is civil war re-enactment. All of them. England, USA, Spain, you name it, I'll recreate it.

A hobby of mine is not going to parties, then wishing I'd gone.

A hobby of mine is match fixing games of tiddlywinks I come across.

A hobby of mine is calculating the price of light.

A hobby of mine is getting lost and being found.

A hobby of mine is buying books by my friends, and then failing to read them. Better than not buying them I suppose.

A hobby of mine is being cancelled, then yelling at my cancellers that it is a privilege to be cancelled as it means I have been listened to, at least once.

A hobby of mine is thinking in telegrams.

A hobby of mine is inviting my friends round for a last supper every Thursday.

A hobby of mine is getting closer in order to see better.

A hobby of mine is wearing the costumes of the lower orders of the metropolis.

A hobby of mine is representing the bully state.

A hobby of mine is worshipping at The Church of the Space Lollipop.

A hobby of mine is thinking about the Byzantine Empire.

A hobby of mine is thinking about the Hanseatic League. (No really, this is true. I don't give a monkeys about Byzantium.)

A hobby of mine is being Bank Holiday handsome.

A hobby of mine is being a Bauhaus pescatarian.

A hobby of mine is spruiking.

A hobby of mine is living in the department store that never sleeps.

A hobby of mine is queuing instead of thinking.

A hobby of mine is ruling from a throne of hash browns.

A hobby of mine is buying myself the damn flowers.

A hobby of mine is withdrawing with style from the chaos (I mean, if you're gonna steal it might as well be from Tom Stoppard).

A hobby of mine is keeping Standard Railroad Time.

A hobby of mine is breaking into the silence.

A hobby of mine is planning a long and prosperous life.

A hobby of mine is reviving the use of outmoded insults, you lolly gagging poltroon!

A hobby of mine is cannibalising failed projects in a forlorn hope to complete others.

A hobby of mine is finding you in these city streets.

A hobby of mine is making every play.

A hobby of mine is hiding in the right back position for most team sports.

A hobby of mine is wittering at clouds.

A hobby of mine is traversing the boundary between being new and being familiar.

A hobby of mine is daydreaming in Chelsea.

A hobby of mine is sleepwalking in Soho.

A hobby of mine is clapping in Clapton.

A hobby of mine is forgetting to wear my sunglasses.

A hobby of mine is calling it an Indian summer well into December.

A hobby of mine is moving a man from point a to point b against his will.

A hobby of mine is poking the bear, though not when they're toileting in the woods.

A hobby of mine is going once round the fair.

A hobby of mine is ignoring the emails from everyone asking for a review or feedback or some sort of further interaction beyond the transaction. You were 5-star honey! Of course you were! Like I'd tell you anything else to your digital face. What kind of mug do you take me for?

A hobby of mine is pretending to be concerned for my dignity when really I don't mind losing it in pursuit of glee, fun, a new crush.

A hobby of mine is lingering over long lunches (hi Jay).

A hobby of mine is stomping.

A hobby of mine is being struck by nouns, inappropriately.

A hobby of mine is the higher banter.

A hobby of mine is dancing the brighter foxtrot.

A hobby of mine is being cited in the most unlikely of places.

A hobby of mine is burning down the house.

A hobby of mine is writing cheques my body can't cash.

A hobby of mine is making notes on blowouts, barbecues, and barbarianism.

A hobby of mine is rejecting the authority of established churches.

A hobby of mine is uniting crowns.

A hobby of mine is being a husband to two kingdoms.

A hobby of mine is observing the conditions.

A hobby of mine is having a convenient store of arms handy within a frontier territory.

A hobby of mine is building over hell, pointing at the bricks and calling it Rome.

A hobby of mine is walking into fire.

A hobby of mine is trying to remember fragments of Shakespeare when I can't sleep.

A hobby of mine is getting loose.

A hobby of mine is being uptight.

A hobby of mine is being a chaise longue for the boy cat.

A hobby of mine is giving blood.

A hobby of mine is waking up at 4.30am with existential dread.

A hobby of mine is making my idiocy appear natural and inevitable.

A hobby of mine is not telling people I love how I really feel, until it is far, far too late.

A hobby of mine is misreading the signs.

A hobby of mine is being elliptical in communication rather than direct.

A hobby of mine is being disappointed when my communications are not correctly parsed, interpreted or otherwise received.

A hobby of mine is resentfully smiling through the idiotic feedback of those who have money and power but no taste or style.

A hobby of mine is annealing.

A hobby of mine is cuckoldry.

A hobby of mine is developing taxonomies of human and social behaviours.

A hobby of mine is relativising sins as offences against taste or style.

A hobby of mine is hustling on the side as if it will mean I thrive in this economy.

A hobby of mine is carrying on as if there isn't an ongoing apocalypse.

A hobby of mine is telling people explaining is a superpower.

A hobby of mine is unintentionally mansplaining.

A hobby of mine is being on the other side of imaginary dialogues with death.

A hobby of mine is conforming.

A hobby of mine is conforming to logic.

A hobby of mine is coming up with scenarios for novels and then never getting round to writing them. Right now, my favourite one of these is telling the story of a man who goes to Edinburgh every January to see the Turner watercolours that are only on display in that month, because that's when the light is low enough to protect them from fading.

A hobby of mine is trying to fit my confessions into sonnets.

A hobby of mine is creating new rituals.

A hobby of mine is treating optimism as a provocation.

A hobby of mine is disrupting the disruptors.

A hobby of mine is being special, progressive, and fun.

A hobby of mine is aggregating slights into melodramas.

A hobby of mine is defusing melodramas into mellow dramas.

A hobby of mine is personality hunting.

A hobby of mine is wishing I'd got famous before the other Rishi.

A hobby of mine is personally visiting ill on my enemies.

A hobby of mine is going faster than is sensible, possible.

A hobby of mine is declaring that my inauthenticity is real.

A hobby of mine is sitting on every available fence.

A hobby of mine is reminding people that technology won't replace taste, unless you get out of the way.

A hobby of mine is democracy.

A hobby of mine is democratising motion.

A hobby of mine is digitising my face so it can be endlessly adapted.

A hobby of mine is Gaussian splatters.

A hobby of mine is saying "Napoleon was right!"

A hobby of mine is watching all nine hours of the 1927 Napoleon biopic while standing up.

A hobby of mine is fomenting revolutions led by squids wearing top hats.

A hobby of mine is wearing a blindfold while eating a pizza with chopsticks.

A hobby of mine is winning various Nobel Prizes.

A hobby of mine is trying to understand the laws of quantum mechanics.

A hobby of mine is solving a Rubik's Cube made out of Play-Doh.

A hobby of mine is wearing a tuxedo.

A hobby of mine is playing with a cat that is actually a sock puppet.

A hobby of mine is forgetting cocktails.

A hobby of mine is The Aviation.

A hobby of mine is searching for partners in crime.

A hobby of mine is trying to turn a partner in innocence into a partner in crime.

A hobby of mine is catastrophizing in a non-linear manner.

A hobby of mine is wringing my hands in the face of distant imperial onslaught.

A hobby of mine is being inspired by Joe Brainard.

A hobby of mine is stopping.

ACKNOWLEDGEMENTS

A hobby of mine is thanking Aaron Kent for indulging my fancies; Jay Owens for the encouragement; and Scott Wortley for the sociability.

LAY OUT YOUR HOBBIES

www.ingramcontent.com/pod-product-compliance
Lightning Source LLC
LaVergne TN
LVHW041310080426
835510LV00009B/940